A World of Computers

Contents

Computers Everywhere	2
Write On!	4
E-mail	6
The Internet	8
Special Needs	10
Shopping at Home	12
Computers in Stores	14
Finding the Way	16
Out in Space	18
Computer Art	20
Fun and Games	22
Index	24

Computers Everywhere

Many people use computers. There are desktop computers and laptop computers. There are even computers that can fit in the palm of your hand.

Do You Know?

The first computers were huge. A computer could take up a whole room!

Write On!

Most writers use computers. They can easily edit text on screen and save and print their work. Computers are also used to create whole books!

Betty is the author of *A World of Computers*.

Kuljit is a book designer.

Do You Know?

The book you are reading now was written, designed, and printed using computers.

Dan is using the Internet to find pictures for the book.

E-mail

People use computers to send e-mail to one another. They can communicate very quickly, whether they are in the same town or in different countries.

E-mails are transmitted through the telephone system. Over long distances, satellites carry the telephone signals.

Do You Know?
E-mail is short for *electronic mail.*

E-mails can include pictures, people's voices, movies, and music.

The Internet

The Internet is used for sending e-mail. You can also find information about almost anything on the Internet. It's like having thousands of books at your fingertips.

People can even connect to the Internet using a cell phone.

Internet cafes are popular all around the world.

Special Needs

Computers help people who have a disability. They help people move, communicate, and learn.

These children can't use keyboards, but they can still use computers.

Shopping at Home

Many people shop on the Internet. They can compare products and prices, order what they want, and pay — all without leaving home!

Computers in Stores

In most stores, the price of every item is listed on a computer. When an item is scanned, its price is shown on the cash register.

Do You Know?
Computers keep track of what has been sold. They tell the store when more goods need to be ordered.

Finding the Way

Navigation computers help people find their way. They show exactly where a ship or plane or car is on Earth. Some cars even have a computer that talks to the driver!

Do You Know?

A navigation computer is called a GPS. This stands for Global Positioning System. The GPS picks up signals from satellites high above the Earth.

A plane's computers help the pilot fly and land the plane safely.

Out in Space

Computers help astronauts find their way through space. Astronauts also use computers to communicate with Mission Control back on Earth.

Computer Art

Computers can be used to create amazing pictures. Some look like they're in 3-D!

These pictures were all created on computers. The artists didn't draw or paint on paper.

Fun and Games

Computer games are great fun. They can be challenging, too! What computer games have you played?

Index

art	20–21
astronauts	18–19
books	4–5
disabilities	10–11
e-mail	6–8
games	22–23
GPS	16
Internet	8–9
navigation	16–17
planes	16–17
satellites	6, 16
shopping	12–13
special needs	10–11
stores	14–15